this only home

poems by
Dennis Cooley

TURNSTONE PRESS

Copyright © 1992 Dennis Cooley

Turnstone Press
607-100 Arthur Street
Winnipeg, Manitoba
Canada R3B 1H3

All rights reserved. No part of this book may be reproduced or transmitted in any form or by any means—graphic, electronic or mechanical—without the prior written permission of the publisher. Any request to photocopy any part of this book shall be directed in writing to the Canadian Reprography Collective, Toronto.

Turnstone Press gratefully acknowledges the assistance of the Manitoba Arts Council and the Canada Council in the publication of this book.

Cover design and illustration: Doowah Design

Text design: Marilyn Morton

This book was printed and bound in Canada by Hignell Printing Limited for Turnstone Press.

Canadian Cataloguing in Publication Data

Cooley, Dennis, 1944-

This only home

Poems.
ISBN 0-88801-164-4

I. Title.

PS8555.O575T4 1992   C811'.54   C92-098029-5
PR9199.3.C65T4 1992

acknowledgements

a note on *this only home*

It was Dec 24, 1989, and I was shopping for Christmas presents. Ran my eye over the sale section in the book store and there was a large book with a brilliant photograph on the cover. *The Home Planet*. Breath-taking photographs of earth, the astonishing beauty of it, huge blue eyeball staring into space. Inside there were more pictures, stunning views of earth, and with them bits and pieces of text, and it all leapt into some place that was ready.

Started that night writing, overwhelmed by what I saw and read. The astronauts—cosmonauts as the Russians call themselves—spoke simply and movingly of their lives in space, and of the lives they looked back to across that blackness. This happened in spite of myself. I was always one of those who found the space business offensive in its worship of power and jingoism, took personal affront, almost, with the hype that spoiled the moon landing. But these astronauts spoke of their children, their grandmothers, gardens in the country, and they wrote so yearningly, so tenderly. Must have written, what? 20 poems that week. Christmas eve, Christmas day, boxing day as we sat in the Winnipeg airport, as the plane took off for a conference in Chicago—the poems came. Poem after poem fell out of the book, found itself under the lovely names and came into those touching voices.

I have revised the poems and added more since—discovering astronomers who poked long glasses into the stars and stirred them around. But I have tried always to catch what for me is a nearly stricken sense of the largeness and the homesickness these people felt, their awe too, in midst of their machines and charts.

But it was that book, *The Home Planet*, more than anything, that set things off and it is that book to which I am enormously indebted. One of the astronauts, Reinhard Furrer, says in it, "I would have wished that after my return people had asked me how it was out there. How I coped with the glistening blackness of the world and how I felt being a star that circled the Earth." I have tried to write what I heard him say, and what I heard others say. Joseph Allen saw the sun come up like thunder, tracked stars till they stopped—found earth. Valeri Ryumin felt as if he was leaving the planet forever and that there was no power that could bring him back. Boris Volynov came back from seeing the sun and moon, the earth, found that he would touch things with trepidation, felt fear that even in his breathing now, its patience, the earth might crack open. Valentin Lebedev—he more than any other—filled his head with poems. They all spoke a poetry so eloquent and so moving I have brought it, gratefully, into *this only home*. I wish I could recite all their names here. They have given me their words and it is to them I dedicate the book.

In addition to *The Home Planet* (Kevin W. Kelley, editor), I have drawn upon the following sources:

Timothy Ferris, *Coming of Age in the Milky Way*
Stillman Drake, ed., *Discoveries and Opinions of Galileo*
Daniel J. Boorstin, *The Explorers*
Galileo Galilei, *Siderius Nuncius*
Ian Ridpath, *Book of the Universe*
David Darling, *Deep Time*
Plato, *The Republic*, trans. Desmond Lee
Edward Harrison, *Darkness at Night*
CBC, "Quirks and Quarks"
Arthur Koestler, *The Sleepwalkers*
Dennis Mammana, *Star Hunters*
Jonathan Weiner, *Planet Earth*

I have also used the *Winnipeg Free Press*. There must have been others but these are the ones I remember.

Several of these poems have appeared in *Border Crossings* and in *Horizons*, or been broadcast over CBC, sometimes in slightly different form. On CBC: "leaving," "the lights of home," "letters," "space walk," "Annie," "thieves of darkness," "lagoon," "home again." In *Border Crossings*: "the starry message," "alluvial," "the beautiful young men," "dried apricots," "it dawns on us," "when i press my face against the darkness," "home again," "the lights of home." In *Horizons*: "stars & stories" and "Newton."

contents

that the world is on fire • 1
blast-off • 4
a room so deep with silence • 5
the other end of starlight • 6
Thomas Digges • 7
departure • 8
night prairie • 10
peeping toms • 11
sight seeing • 14
how on earth • 15
predators • 17
felt • 18
the lights of home • 19
all the seasons • 20
Annie • 22
above and below the moon • 24
twice smitten • 26
zodiac • 28
kids • 29
transfusion • 30
polar navigation • 31
the starry message • 32
east of eden • 33
dawn • 35
gravity • 37
holy cow • 38
the swimmers • 39
cinderella • 41
star making • 44

creatures falling out of the stars • 45
intravenous space • 47
we return • 49
the beautiful young men • 51
at every turn • 53
delta • 55
"some large tired bird" • 56
when I press my face against the darkness • 58
Newton • 59
Madagascar • 61
the new telescope • 62
shuttle cock • 64
inner ear • 66
the omega horses wear on their feet • 67
it had always seemed so • 69
new as babies • 71
stars & stories • 73
thieves of darkness • 75
foetal • 77
lagoon • 78
walking at night the gravel beach • 79
they're gonna make a big star • 81
what he sees • 83
polar light • 85
boxing day • 87
viscosity • 89
my eye • 90
space walk • 91
visitations • 93
strolling in the garden • 94
preface • 96

bonnie • 99
home game • 100
rock pickers • 103
it dawns on us • 104
our old man's a dustman • 106
Magellan, all the stars • 107
held • 110
navigation • 111
the squeeze earth puts you in • 112
impaled on a trajectory • 114
the men in the moon • 116
the orbits of planets • 117
alluvial • 118
Kepler • 119
they wow the earth • 123
vacuum • 124
leaving • 126
nemesis • 128
this only world • 130
passing • 132
Apollo II • 133
dried apricots • 136
theres Gary • 138
letters • 139
foundry • 141
scanning the heavens • 142
hatched • 143
& you have been drunk • 144
space colony • 147
Eugene Cernan • 148
home again • 150

that the world is on fire
very large stars have a
short life that ends violently
—like rock stars

Heraclitus was right that
wonders in the sky close & open
never cease gas clouds arc into stars
into protostars, first, condensing

some bloop out, swim dark seas one line
red dwarf   red giant   white dwarf   black dwarf
some nudge into a more gnarled story
yellow dwarf   yellow giant   red giant   blue giant
slide into the first line then into white dwarf black dwarf
another string twists, fuse into spectacular violence
no one can ignore blue dwarf   blue giant   yellow
supergiant   red supergiant gathers itself, epic hero,
the gigantic explosion we call supernova

the wonderful names they follow, on their way to death

the story takes you into marvel, lends you vertigo
supernovae heave into pulsars and black holes
heavy elements dropping from them across the heavens
it could be a hailstorm, crushes space
debris falls into us our bones crusted with stars

& seven have been sighted & written down
125 B.C. Hipparchus watches a new star
forming in the sky his eye his mind
till he must have been blind, almost, with it, in him
it is 1054 and the Chinese see and follow
"a guest star" in the sky, guest still
its remnants a swollen tangle of gasses
ghost we call the Crab Nebula

& then stable stars skies that come & go
for centuries known to watchers until
a rash of boiling light & tilted heads
1572 Tycho Brahe reads its braille
it burns through spots the night
takes with it the framed stars
the membrane we were warm in
then the comet of 77 & Kepler
sticky with blood the century ends
crosses appear in hands & feet the trees
hot & brittle as if a fire had passed
though it is worms & there is
talk of torture & burnings

then Kepler, dazzled, his star, in 1604,
and five years later, 1609, Galileo
stumbles at his vigil pigeon-toed with
what he sees—a third

        three in a lifetime
       the sky turned to fire
            & then the earth
      on a rack its whole body
         ripped & bleeding
   we call the Thirty Years' War

   then nothing, not a glimmer,
      except one, small peek,
        then Feb 23, 1987,
    an observatory in Chile
one more looms
out from the Magellanic Cloud
the Portuguese sailed into
three and a half centuries before
and now they take out the needles
that held it, spinning, this light unknits
out of the blur sailors rubbed from their eyes

   it is 150,000 years after
   hydrogen sleeps in boxes boxers make
   bides its time is it time
   to burn everything off the earth
   a grassfire no wall can stop, or well

          the small scars in us
      staring into a huge empty bubble

blast-off

        the perimeter people
  dark silhouettes
the dark curve they form
    & hover at

how speed carries
      the rim
  they are on
          feel
    when the rockets let go
        air & earth
  shaking

        the roar   in them
      silhouettes into the sky
    all the people
dark shadows
                early dawn
      the sky on fire
          people
    turning on the edges
        their faces
  into light
                taking pictures
  sticks whose heads they lean to
    dark people
      pale sun
              /shaking
  eating the fire

a room so deep with silence

  a room so deep with silence
  we tumbled through our stomachs
  something folding in

   we were children there
   this huge swimming pool
   without a murmur
   we floated & bobbed the world

floated by no not a rattle
or a ball nothing like that

a garden we wondered in wandered at
everything untainted we tended
the way children bend & peer

everything tinted a stain so new
so clear it could have been wet

   the whole earth brighter than crayons
    & more varied
   we wandered in & out
   played in the stars grew we found
   our voices sleepier somehow
     ,more awake

felt we could reach out &
   touch the globe
so touchingly near
  so far away in night

the other end of starlight

that light is lost when it leaves
the stars when finally it reaches
us it touches our face provisional
as breath you fall asleep
and where it came from may be gone

that light from your face lights
on my face lights all our faces
light up that is all

        that and knowing
        by the time it does
        when i feel it light
        you may be gone
        all the light gone
        all the switches burnt out

Thomas Digges

This Orbe of Starres Fixed Infinitely vp Extendeth Hit Self in
Altitvde Sphericallye, and Therefore

Immovable the Pallace of Foelicitye Garnished with Perpetvall
Shininge Gloriovs Lightses Innvmerable

Farr Excellinge Ovr Sonne both in Qvantitye and Qvalitye the Very
Covrt of Coelestiall Angelles
Devoyd of Greefe and Replenished with Perfite Endlesse Joye the
Habitacle for the Elect

The Orbe of Satvrne Makinge His Revolvtion in 30 Yeares
The Orbe of Jvpiter Makinge His Periode in 12 Yeares
The Orbe of Mars Makinge His Revolvtion in 2 Yeares
The Great Orbe Carringe This Globe of Mortalitye
His Circvlar Periode Determineth Ovr Yeare
The Orbe of Venus Rovleth Rovnd in 9 Monthes
The Orbe of Mercvry in 8 Dayes
The Sonne

—adapted from Edward Harrison, *Darkness at Night*, 20.

departure

                    wham & we're in
                        slam slam slam
                  someone's at the door
                  only you don't answer

                  they batten the hatch
                            that's it

      lower ourselves
       into the couch
       crouch there on
           the ledge
          dark makes
    primates who are
             about
       to stand up &

        no not be counted
         nor count either
       though we do that

                    :stand up &
                    wish we will
              one day once more
                          stand

some thing is taking us
it will paste us
doughy moon a child has
cut clumsily into life
& glued there with love

        unable to withstand
            the slightest
                weight

      on the way here saw
ducks swim away in the small pond
      where Atlantis lifts off
        white bird on its back
    & someone's made a picture

wonder if we are cut out
                      for this
     if we are forever
                      cut off
       from home

night prairie

        an immensity i saw once
          : night on the prairies

an enormous sky far as you can see
the earth lets go in yeast
a shrill sun filled
     with insects   & wind

  : all of it — scooped out
a huge excavation of light
      so that darkness pours

      seas of it
    at night fills the land

& at the top
    the heavy water
    hard as iron
       where the torch blows through
    : millions of bright insects
           :

peeping toms

hour after hour watching darkness under darkness
their loneliness hunched at the pinholes
through sighting tubes their eyes revel
night draped over their shoulders
the expectant way they fold it, the studied ease
reveals sights that keep them peering up
into the flimsy fabric the skirts stars are sewn to

       it is not what you think no
       they do not want their names in stars
       not only, want something more, turn
       their courtly attentions to the sky
       come back night after night

all the squinting at the eye pieces
pawing years from books fawning for favour
the all-night vigils a romance that makes their breath
stop Kepler Brahe Galileo cannot take their eyes off
              what they see takes their breath
              away fogs up the lenses does it
              take away their very souls
   Newton diddling in alchemy Kepler and Brahe
   casting horrorscopes in court courting favour

   but this, these lights every night
   Tycho Brahe in his tight circles
   amazed stops dead even his mineral nose his first
   nose slicked off in a boyhood duel
          even the nose he oils stops
    his long handled moustache & arrogance
  stop too lean with him against
the wondrous instruments he swings under the stars
"as if astonished and stupefied" he writes
his lover's words cannot take his eyes away
cannot believe his eyes cries that he might be confirmed

      Kepler too is swept off his feet Kepler
      squints through myopia tries to rub
       multiple vision out of his eyes
      his search for the five perfect solids
       planets run unsoiled between

he sees "with incredible and ravishing delight"
peers out of smallpox his son disappeared to death
inside women burning his mother barely escaping
the bloody crosses that fill Hungary sink into bodies
like graves Johannes Kepler scabby runt whips himself
  with self-loathing and misery and rags
    scrapes stories off dead skin reads
his own birth chart wraps himself in conjunctions

      these men late at night, neglectful,
        cast their roving eyes over the night
their families sleeping wives dreaming neglect
Kepler looks out a small window in a dreary marriage
rubs it and rubs it, tries to clear a small spot
Brahe braced drunken against his array of globes & quadrants

they are ravished in nocturnal emissions

               Kepler longs to hear a music box
               an amatory world where bodies
               roll slow around other bodies
      silent and solemn, relief from the screams
      the vicious dwarf Jepp, Brahe shouting
      throws scraps to (throws scraps to him, Kepler
      dreaming beautiful bodies which as they move
              together   /quicken
        apart, take on torpor

    no wonder they hold glass to their eye
      study a dark lady who wears lights
        on her breast the milky way
        they squat under muddy lives
   want beauty want grace court romance
surcease from war, witches crackling to death

                    all night long they kneel
                    behind infra-red eyes

sight seeing

a ship's wake
      so distinct in the Indian Ocean
so astonishingly simple
      it hits you
the way driving into British Columbia
      that time
the sky absolutely empty
      so empty you could
see forever
        & your head too ,empty
      & then
            a vapour trail

it was as if someone
  were drawing an elegant
eyelash across the sky
  this perfectly smooth
            face

        all this in the middle of noise
        the radio, the car moving

how on earth

how on earth we stand on earth
throw our voices to the top of blackness
wait for them to find the stars
for voices to veer back shake loose
other voices from the furthest corners
voices that are high and nasal perhaps
they have heard and call back
they could come, thick velocity
from a muted megaphone

how all alone we stand
call out to the stars sing
to the stars ourselves in night
do what for all our time we have done
a million years we have stood
wetting our feet on the oceans
we have cast our voice upon the waters
steered them out onto darkness
how silent the stars little ships
seem even when our ears grow enormous
and there are whispers from space

again and again we have dropped
our voices among the stars
spoke suddenly, unknowingly,
when other lights drifted
graceful paths the silence
the softness of their moving
from night to night

if they saw us floating so blue
so white on the vastness of space
would they know we are here on the shores
on clear dark nights watching
the stars painted on plates
where they wheel and swing wires
bicycle over us, the stars on wires

for ten thousand centuries people
have kept time by the stars juggled
their dreams stunned with the sweep
have seen stars called to earth
sometimes we have lost our breath
the tides have risen in us our eyes gone
utterly dark we have understood they speak
sun and moon and rain Hammurabi felt on his face
the seasons wobble sweetly around us
all the plants and animals they drag behind
the breath we take from the nearest star

predators

bang they shut the dark
        bang bang
  we are dropped in
our breath
       padlocked
something has come over us
something predates us or predicts

somewhere on the top of the castle
beneath us a rocking & hissing
              & in us
the machinery chugging away

     & then something comes down
     around us they start to
          close us up
     something dead & terribly alone

        when they pull
          the hood
        down over us
      we are left
       waiting
     on the scaffold
          on god's wrist
          the writ of god

   bang bang they say
  bang bang

     you are good
     as dead
  they said

felt

    like that cow
        jumped o
            ver the
                moon

            out there
          the dark
         lowing
        the yell
ow cow
browsing
on stars

the lights of home

night and we cross the Atlantic
back from America cellular clouds
sheepskin slippers scattered
sleepy on bluecarpets

where has everyone gone
we have come back
from America where the Belcher Islands
are wound in white sugar candy
the sharpest mountains are more
like molars than anything

the first snow   -skin on the land
rivers dark as blood on the back
my hand in the wrists is an estuary

earth a giant heart bright heart
we circle and circle round
the oceans our heart swishes
and little fires everywhere
matches in carpets only brighter
                         & beautiful
our hearts are lined with it

                         & then
a huge star brilliant snowflake
light skeined in the veins
thousands & thousands of veins
something alive and inconsolably beautiful

I had seen Moscow

all the seasons

small frogs
        in blue plasma
we went out in spring
          everything stirring
    we were green lamps
        in the breeze

        sailed across summer
& the fall
      flew into winter

          :   at first
   whiteness
& then green
        & then gold

& then whiteness once more
      the cold
       sun spent
the way we would sway
  over the changes

    the way they would
    free or freeze us

the year like a hand
        waving, slowly

```
        only now
    its silence
                moving
       away
                in the
other direction
            —says Anatoli Berezovoy
```

Annie

   thinking of you   Annie
      earth there some
         where
a cuticle of light

     sun I like to think will
        manicure
              in morning
earth moving you in sleep
turning our capsule moving

       find only the blackest black
          I ever saw
        earth complete
      inked in all the brackets
        full & some
             thing sinks
     a racket you feel
       but do not hear

    utterly blank ,
       blink & it's
still there
       silent as death it is
      colder than icicles
          in your hands Annie
the bicycle we rode & a cut
on the thumb earth has become
      numb maybe

        Annie   older
   than everything in your heart
        & as young

            everything is written
  or nothing

  in the dark we track
         the stars link them
)bracelets)
      until the stars
(stop

            :that's earth
              that's you
          blocking the light
                  carbon
       paper I cannot read
          or write
        home to you

above and below the moon

when we were under the stars
slid into place year after year
snapped snow & cold into place
turned plants into seeds
blew ships in season
brought calves to time
roots out of sleeping

swam into night
saw first light scattered
over our faces felt
rain fall out of the stars

the very firmament a sweet new ferment
stars gliding over wet film

the stones they told we learned
to hear the rocks at Stonehenge
stars & planets a ferris
wheel around them wear
their clockworks on the outside

sailors sliding off the edge of the sea
hearts sliding open to fear wide as wind
& later other men with bits of glass

now within the stars it seems
though one day
we might some say
seed the deep furrows of space
seal the furnaces shut around the sun

      i cannot think it likely
      or wish it ever for now
      we cannot read them
      they can not bring us

what happens when earth goes
    the birds slicing across
            strange wild cries
the wetness of animals when they open
    warm air & when they are
let out of winter kick their heels like kids

      all the lids lifted & the songs
    escaped where birds chip songs out of air
      the metallic blue turnips grew under
      the whole earth loud with bud & blood

everywhere around us strange stars
we are blown across stars
storm swarm the thin cold waters
strange constellations come out
turn out of time fall out in silence
from stories we always told ourselves
found comfort in, felt at home among

stars swim now strange phosphorescence
leashed to wind sun blows out
    : fish in dark winters
Pluto in his dark root cellar
never imagined never thought to keep

twice smitten

how Galileo hungry for something
hounds Kepler into the forest hot on the trail
wedges his mind in among the stars
is smitten is a driven man
bends on the fulcrum his passion fixes
pries the stars loose levers the earth free

        until he stands on earth
            a huge blue eye
          cold marble he holds
    in the jar his mind has become
             stuffs the stars in
             and shakes them

     how like Blake he rails
       curses fools & blockheads
        slashes at their romance
he has seen the world in his mind's eye
it is not green nor pleasant
it is a grain of sand

    all night Galileo watches
    the silk robe slip from a smiling moon
    sees as he woos her
             her face turn
                away
         from him
             her sad and wan face
   the scabs & blotches

Galileo hungry for something
            disappointed lover
stands watch over the stars
                faithful as Gatsby
       in love

zodiac

                            tarnish of night
sky

               dip
     into the   tank

                            the dark
                                    ness

       emerge :

                     : clean
         as silver
jewellery   :
         dripping cold
                          as memories
              your memories

:
     of me

kids

    those summer nights
             your wife & kids
  thikk thik   bugs on screens

gluey bodies of children
sleep sticks them onto night
they click in pale petals

        call from their dreams
           thick with it,   the heat

  earth inside its thin bubble
          , breathing
  so thin you gasp in terror

you lying on the ceiling
you touch the face of
        a sky
    tenderly
as you would a child
        horrified
as if you were a child
      you touch the face

transfusion

        the great lakes greet us
      their grief where they dangle
       from the long arm the St.
          Lawrence grips &
       teaches us we too might

  touch things be touched by them
grope into the stone heart of a continent
     feel it flowing up our arms
    the way Scott felt it (starting
     at the Lakehead & before it
    something stuck in its throat

polar navigation

       so sure the stars, so near
     the solan goose must also cruise
by bleeps & blips in a sonar noose
on automatic pilot through shipwrecked stars
purple as new wounds grey as old pain
solar panels adjust its steerage

    all the stars its brain compacts
       map the stars it steers by

a solenoid brain silent & solemn
a submarine in the north atlantic
the stars themselves perhaps no more solid

         somewhere in their eyes relay switches
              click/
                        on & off
on the marquees they are flashing
the coming attraction on the far
      side of earth

         the moon
   the stars the sun
        running lights on its voyage
              all the way out
     & back

the starry message

it is dark when I lift the tube
dark as if I am in a closed cell
a closet my clothes hang in, smoky
the light I have snuffed

I have put together the two lenses
I Galileo Galilei have
arranged for light where concave meets
convex eye glasses brought together
the right way, easy if you know how

hear the pigs grunt
look into silence then settle
the sounds of drunk lovers in the lane
and I turn my face to the sky
night breeze and the wet smells

east of eden

        earth they saw its blueness
        come out of the earth itself
        bluing in laundry, that fresh

    earth an opal they could wear
    on the finger birth stone earth stone

not now says Mr. Underwood (from Texas)
the earth so smudged the photos are no longer

so bright or beautiful as they were
25 or 30 years ago

      Lake Chad the size of Lake Erie
      has totally dried up the Sahara
      sprawls across it

          across the oceans ships clean
          their tanks scrawl ink
          behind them it streaks
          into the underworld

we are bad house keepers
the blue eye, once a light house
fuzzy now as the flannel we sleep in
something in its eye, weeps for our harm
we all are in the same boat now

earth a blue iris is filming over
ships a tear in its eye
the earth is starting to go blind
we do not want to be homeless
adams whirling in space
exiles from the garden

want to turn season to season
watch the fish and the flowers
feeding on stars

dawn

    5 miles per second we move
        : :   freckles in time

                    & then dawn
                        yawns
      or no
            / lifts

      a purple plate
there at the rim of the world
       & there is a red
   that pinches under

        lines sharp as linen
        cuffs on your sleeve

        sun spiders in
           on to your walls
  throws lines
sweet as raspberries

      drift through

    shadow/
                  light
  shadow
     /light
                     shadow

hard to tell are we
washed or swallowed

;   flies
their speckled quickness

sleep on your eyes
& flicker

gravity

    have felt stars swarm my face
    my heart swim in my hand have
    heard what Newton said the greater
    the mass the stronger the pull
    the further the distance the less attraction

        know only i am in a stone
          I am a stone
        a child swings round &
        round as a moon a child tugs
        from far away holds me here
          keeps my thoughts
        from swarming
            from flying   off

my daughter on the other end
the cord stronger than gravity
feel the cord how it vibrates,
        heart in my hand

holy cow

```
                    hey   rune
            diddle              the
        fiddle                      for
         the                       straight
          rat                       went
         and                         wish
         the                          the
       riddle                         and
         the                          dark
         now                          such
      jumped                          see
         over                          to
          the                       laughed
             moon              bat
                   the   little
```

the swimmers

        evening
      so beautiful
     it is a wet pasture
   we tether to us
   fear it might stray

purple sky an ocean
millions and millions swim
we flail & shout to one another
come on in the water's fine

the high seas could be enormous
     & are
  still
so huge you cannot speak

     watch the moon :
       aluminum ball
        float to the top
   our faces turn toward

     fear everything
   the moon sky ourselves
    might be so torn
     may be so ript
    off drift off into
    garbage & death

```
         the whole sky so   bare
      so barely held   on the end of our hopes
                   we feel it   might go
                              might   float
         away   easy as ice   flows
                              final   as ice




                where all the life
             guards have gone
                              who is
                   watching

                   all the swimmers
                        where they fail
                   in high lone strokes
```

cinderella

so near i touch the gas
you drift in and shine
as you shine i admit it
i too emit a glow of my own
brighter than grass after rain
our bodies from love

so far away you swirl sail
away on clouds of gas and dust
you could be a galleon or at least a clipper
& you tack across the big dipper
my slipper tucked gallantly in your pocket

is this what you want all that dust
the way it furls about you & you cough
your hacking & lustless cough
it only fuels your mad rushing away
you could be a victorian bursar
you have become tubercular & you have
absconded with my affections
or worse the start of
something big

               the velocity of our separation
             moving outward awkward with stars
                   and between them fear
                 in the rifts i will keep moving
             escape the way you pull always away
                   think you may never fall back
                 on my body the sweet gravity
                 comes and goes and so do
             words we whirl between us up &
             down the twisted strings kids spin
                   between their hands
                      until they pile up
                       7-deep in drifts

the way you glow there
a famous fuzzy thing
how lights on christmas trees go
when you almost close your eyes
or i am sweeping the kitchen

                      admit it mr.
                  cinderella   fella
                        yr ok so far but
                  one day you perhaps
                  will spend a lifetime
                  burning in some state
                    a relative constancy
              weeping i will drift through
                      your dust & shine
              brushing the stars from your eyes
        where they seep more leaky than an old toilet

in the meantime you perhaps
could think of me sleeping away
stars in your eyes some sweet glue
keeping you true to me knowing
come what may though you will say
"with" you are finally stuck on
me you should thank
your lucky stars

star making

massive blue spots form clumps
that's where fresh stars start
hot young stars blown into space

flesh is bruised & it flashes
into existence its blue flesh
baby blue flesh shows
bright as Venus in morning
an aether dream we breathe in
babies breath on the night

all the new stars circulate
red giants pulse on the edges
they are the hot hearts of creation
       foetal, they feed us

our ripped hearts our flesh
regions where things are made
       & unmade

       in the cold reaches
       that keep us apart
       matter keeps coming together
       coming into awareness of itself
       something fatal in that

something we could
       live & drown in

creatures falling out of the stars

are they as some believe
ourselves returned from the stars

somewhere there is always
a gap in time they could be

ourselves come back to our
selves spiralled inside selves
      homey as shoelaces
the way snails build sound in shells
and they live inside the shellac
they put on their music boxes

            some times they make
            love to women one woman
            said she climbed the stars
            with them at night the stars were
            theatres where they rehearsed
            our coming their coming too

      came back with stars
      in her head she said
she knew where there is vastness
so vast you feel as if you were
falling forever their home
      she knew where
      they are they were
known to her before
astronomers tuned
toward them she showed
where they would find them
galaxies no one had seen before

we are ourselves
returned to ourselves
make love to mothers
lovers children aeons older
and younger drawn
home in love they come
back to us we come
back to our senses

no longer beside ourselves

    she said the lady
   whose sons came back
    made love to her
filled her with stars
     till they were falling out of her
  head her hands over
   flowing with stars

witches with wet light in our heads
creatures falling out of the stars
   drawn home in love
    we call them back call back
Odyssean are they sailors
in those black black oceans
whose shores we stand watch at
stirred by the silent roar
   the echoes of stars
bright fishes we pull
    from our dreams

intravenous space

    spun out in spring
             season to season
    sun so strong so unsparing
      the clouds behind us
             coming undone
      one by one, only fast
        very fast
    spin backwards off the skein
    we skim the translucent skin

  it is when you were a kid in an elevator
        you were new from the farm
  and you left your stomach on the ground

turn now in your electric breath :

   earth birth death rain light
clouds lightning night water blue
     sun storm wind ice rivers

many stars blue stars everywhere
more silent than a phone call
           that never comes
the mole on the back of Juri Kagarin
iridescence walks across your thoughts
    across the sky
           glimmer   ,faintly
   sky steep as a jar

dream of falling out of the sky out of the sun
the way people dreamt once
        meteorites were gods, visiting
only you feel more like a homing pigeon
you want to go home find your way back

    why do you think looking out
            earth is a bathtub
            and you are a starfish
            starved for home
the piercing way it comes upon you
time falls upon you knocks your breath out

                      shaky as heart beat
                hung in intravenous space

we return

                      all our days

and beneath our gaze whales seals buffalo
migrate across great canyons of moving
migraines they might be in some cosmic brain
except for the beauty the sweep they swim in

    we weep have been away
we have grazed have braided the cosmos grazed
on light on darkness that fell upon us
wild as lightning days from heat let out

sudden as great doors closing and then opening
followed little blips of light small as decimals
our capsules were and our hearts contained
winds and rain beneath us and we may be

a little crazed now from an airless time
            -but we come back
   flying and we are afraid

we might feel on our mouths
                almost the infinite
beauty of earth, gem germ garment
we wear our brothers our sisters
filled with terror with infinite
love for this our earth some find dismal
                        & final

       every second stars dying
                stars being
       born in memories our brains orbit

    novae boiling away in distant beauty
  every second star moving to death or life

   in these our small and infinitesimal lives

the beautiful young men
in their flying machines

Leonardo in his huge & crashing
machine rose for a moment
in the raw morning light all the hinges
      the whole row going full
      tilt sounded so much
as if a mill started up
or pigeons their small
engines running on hot
how creaky & wooden they lift
their arms his mind their wings
they all are sore he is sure
it will work

      searching for air for pins
      in the air he might get   hold on
      the wind an invisible ladder to god
      might swerve or pivot might
      serve him into the empyrean

      dressed in elegant ribbed wings
          Leonardo is a bird
Leonardo preens his pinions
      he is flying to heaven
wants to cruise among stars
         drink down the sun

Leonardo disentangling himself
darkness heavy as seaweed
hangs on his scheme
Leonardo dangling
on darkness
falling
down

at every turn

    sounds wrong but
    earth is
            impasto

 volcanoes -
       wet pottery
   knife work of a painter
            the fluid wrist
how fluent it all is

snow white beauty of typhoons
Cape Cod dressed in blue nearly blue
         as the ocean
    hooks into the water
      & holds on
  for dear life

the utter surprise in seeing
    they got it right
    the maps were right

          space on your shoulder
        looks over
you on the end of a wrench
 you lean into & you are

     turning
    around a nut
among unblinking planets

no sound tracks to guide us
no kettle drums no cathedrals there
are no tricks or special effects
no impresarios just the crackle
in your ears your blood
              dreams there
blood has its own drama of light

in front the Bahama Islands
            float in blue satin
                  her slip is
    sometimes green
               a queen
              you love
   to touch

delta

       millions of years life creeps
out, filigrees, silts out in the tall grass
               it splits where it is spilt
   fills into new wrists   new hands
     life vessels through the back of your hand
your wrist, so easy to slash open

         the mouth of the miss
              issippi you lean over &
           it is sipping
        there it is
                :a spinach leaf
    that's what it looks like
        ribs & greens
         . cooked

   it's plain it is cooked
       we all can see it
          floats there
     on top
a daub
    of sour cream

people talking about space
     & us in it
  empty space the species
streams into, filling its crooked veins

"some large tired bird"

        glass turns   to plasma
        this   is an ocean
        we are flying   in fire

shudder when we scud through
        bump bump bump
rotten roads in Moscow
break out in frost boils
& we are not even back

        & then
                      . faces
      at the porthole faces
      beautiful faces my god and the
      sudden weight of earth
clouds sweet as you imagine
        home is
ocean of wind &
        rain
              after so long
    wet rain on our faces
        or is it snow we feel
        as if we are struggling
        out of bed or dreams
            we are glued in

      even the helicopter
      when it lands

  cluck cluck cluck cluck
its loud wings on its back as though
it were a lost angel as if
it were about to hatch
or round us up for lunch
some large tired bird brooding
     over us

  "dear earth how good you feel
    sitting on my shoulders"

when I press my face against the darkness

      at the end when something goes
      wrong I press my face against the darkness
      something passes over my mind like water

my daughter then Dmitriki's son
fresh-cheeked as skaters
on the subway that day they sat
side by side all the mothers
the cousins all the lovers and friends
look out look worried & laughing &
      look, there it is

      earth spinning its blue wool
      blue as a field in flax and cotton
        you can see its breath
      it is sliding away there and I
      think how this is so fine
      this could go on forever

      after I am gone my children and
      their children and their children after
      all the children the winds speed
      how all the seeds will be

      earth will be gliding away
            slow & easy
      earth on the back porch of space
      dings away like an ice-cream vendor
      the pace the peace of gamma rays
      rocking away earth everybodys
      gramma rocking away the old lady
      going at it till the end of time

Newton

        saw how it spread
     beautiful as contagion
       from the edge it arced
      sun broke through fell out
      the bright oblongs saw it
burst into spectrum through his head
the heady speculations ached him

this when he unprismed light
   & was puzzled how did it break
     & fall so like a sky
      when rain falls out
the purity of what it passes through

stars refracted there reflected his mind
the concave mirror he gathered starlight in
the tube sight fell down & once there once seeing
the stars could never get out
     till the span opened
      beautiful as a hand, so fresh
      the sky could be rinsed clean
         he couldn't help it
        they opened his eyes
          his eyes opened
wide as the wind between stars

Newton on shore listening at his front door
the faint roar the fountain spraying light
picks pebbles rubs shells sweeps water
with his eyes skips his thoughts
over the waters wondering
how starlight can warp
fall so dazzling
in lights
all day
long
&

Madagascar

    is green the ocean
    red with silt

from where the forests were
torrents of green the earth
in torment bleeds away
the water stiff with blood

the new telescope

how he puts together glass
feels them on his eye his thumb
chooses bumps curves hollows
wraps them in a tube, their physics
locks them in with the light
inside the wooden tube light seals
the light forms washers

    he makes the light
    fit them thinks how
      light slips
   over the lens
    sweet oil
  the smooth molecules
  the roundness of light
  little worlds every one
  he polishes on his thoughts
  sweet as olive oil

    swivels his dreams
   toward the sky his eye
 pivots inside a wooden tube

:

:

                        breath gone
          the shock

                 lights fall through
                    onto dreams
when the moon caves in
everything cracked
everything splintered

      who could have seen
      who now can believe

            the fire we fall away from
               a sky full of fire
               the sky is falling
                 into his mind
            into frightful stories he will be told
                the rest of his life

shuttle cock

                    relatively speaking
        you have been bad you have
                shuttled me   /snottily
  back & forth   back &forth
shot me to & fro in your weaving
          till im damn near
     shot   /or shagged
                & so forth

        i woof for the warp
in time you shut & wrap me in
            that makes me
  some kind of tweeter   or woofer
      now i know your ins & outs
your warped views of time   /& space

```
A gantry is a movable
structure used for erecting
and servicing a rocket
prior to launch.
```

                    & even after
            you baby you send me
      (on your booster) into or in to your ambit
                as an opening gambit
      i snuffle & shuffle back & forth
      eyes a blink & ruddy antennae
      worried on your word you keep me
                    when i come in for a lunar
      landing or a docking rudder air
      brakes shuddering under wraps & hanging
                you are so cock
            sure you can

                        tread on me
                        thread the eye
                        on darkness

inner ear

    once you have been
               there
      all the blood

    your head brooded
        as nightbirds
       with blood
         your life floats
           in arrears

        & you have seen
sun   moon   stars
    the earth

        you come back
           almost afraid
  to touch
       any thing

     wanting more than
        anything
      to touch

            your ear a shoe
            full of blood

the omega horses wear on their feet

    whole galaxies, coarse sugar
    stuck to glass so thin it is molten
    when pions muons neutrinos were
        & hadrons

        how when it has ticked away
        for awhile it begins to feel itself
          pulling & pulling apart
          click click its cells click
           another billion miles
    neural tissue strung across nothing
    but small scarves of heat a faint
warmth that bathes things as they float off

        matter from matter pulling away
          a drift through helium
        that glowed once with heat

    astronomers thinking this could have
started from nothing started to come unglued

        how after awhile it hauls itself back
    offended, almost, only it feels nothing
           returns a huge elastic
          skin stars grown inside
       begins to gather its thoughts

it is a small blip of matter
anti-matter never got nature forgot
to cancel, check out,
a balloon in the side of creation
it has spoken to matter spoken into it
spoken it into existence

how what it says condenses into
wild outbursts & it carries
-270°C , 3 degrees above
absolute zero

we are what is left over
we are an afterthought
and will perish with the stars

how I feel away from you
wanting you so much now
I could pull myself back
hand over hand along
the sticky strings
and when we're back

pop into something new
something slippery past the lip of time
a bottle when a bather strikes out
& blows her loneliness into it

or a spider,
throws her threads
onto the dark sea
hoping

it had always seemed so

       stuffed so crowded with air
                  & clouds so full
       with possibilities with stories
       so many stones they were unending

the stars where we stood so far
in the night its tar & so near
so small for all their magnitude
               earth there
& we were reassured as your small
daughter may have been once when you would
               lift & hold her
& she would try to touch the moon

                but not this
                  (not this)
                how could we have known

earth speeding away
          swirls speeding
inside your heart with love
              & terror
       you could hold
in your hand or put on your finger
         until it seemed   , almost
             it could
   drop   out of sight

                         our stricken selves
              trailing behind

```
    the way you lose
              yourself
          when someone
                   you have always known
    steps
         across your life
              sudden with grace
                    you never saw
            or knew before

    never knew you knew
                 & likely will not see again
                         ever in your life
```

new as babies

        and when we do
  come back
    out of dark & cold so fierce
      it could knock you over
         we climb
to the air   lock
    head first
       turn our   selves up
side down to
    enter
            feet first

this takes   all our force
our hearts rotating the earth rotating
our hearts rotating the earth our hearts
wait until we are blue in the face

    and when at last we pop back
    into the blue membrane
    aerials burnt off in re-entry
        our ears burning
    lie trembling inside the ball
    moon dust on its skin
    a field, squawking like a duck,
                it seems

    only we are small we are
    small voices in snow
    march would melt with whispers

        & then april
    watery wind at the window
              is a siren &
       rain
rinses us we rise
     risen
          new as babies
   wrinkled with weight

stars & stories

how the Greeks looked
out & saw themselves
written in stories stars
told in constellations, stars together,
joined together, 88 of them
my dictionary says, and it gives
the marvellous names
Callisto Taurus Europa Serpens Ganymede
Pegasus the Pleiades Lupus Aquila Hydra

but do we not add
are there no more, ever,
are all the stars told
so constant as 88 and yet
the ancient Chinese saw 300

locked together neat as bones did they
see our ends in stellar storms
bones & tongues
burnt out

how we look out &
the electric stars speak
their hiss & crackles speak
our deaths their deaths
the whole galaxy running
out of gas bursts into flame
Earth burnt or frozen
to absolute darkness
a fleck perhaps with other debris
in the bottom of a black sack
nothing leaves, ever

how when we marvel at the configurations
a tablecloth laid on the sky soft as wish
each night bright buttons macraméd in
or sitting there sparkling as glasses
every continent rimmed with lights
bright sugar they see from space

a back yard, a mother & father
a small child on whose eyes light sprinkles

    the utter desolation no more
   oceans no more snow no eyes
    light touches off no more
   moments when warm bodies meet
   babies wake or call from sleep no
     more food from the oven
   no more children who try to reach
the moon no more bones under their stones
    ringing in earth's diurnal turn
   no more voices that trickle into matter
& out of matter tickle stories no more moons
  or suns no more coffee in the morning

   what good does it do knowing
    there is no god or goddess
    the eye of god poked out
  god's word in the end is silence

thieves of darkness

what can I tell you of this darkness
that it is iron only we float through
Orion cold as glass they store gasses in
and you are sucked into them at a touch
your inner ear bewildered

that it is an onion we are ions inside
& track its rings faithful as bottle collectors
as jewellers with their tricks & music boxes
except we hear no music no smells

    that it is a black sack
    we have untied
      & fallen in
to sun & moon & stars
   birds some hunters bagged
   that in it we are seamen
    swim or swarm
    stars semen eggs

birds whose eyes have been poked out
we sing to the dark call to the sun
rickets breaking out from our bones
    brittle as bricks
our bones break out from want of sun
the splotches we have become
is it sunspots flare our skin

            that it clicks or chills or warms
            us to know we are seamen, or worms
                on a dark dark sea
              that spreads before & speeds

                      something slings the sun past
                            a hot rock
                         in awful whizzes
                monstrous marbles we marvel & shrink from

                                only we
              cannot hear this
                  is not Daedalus dead
                  his flimsy racket broken
                                strings & all
                            the flames the rickety
                            wind sun blew by him
                              in wax & feathers
                he could be a yellow jacket

                  the terrible vertigo
                  the green spinning
                        at the end the rocket's red glare

                      we seek and make ourselves
                    sick we are in the dark I am afraid
                    this blue dream of wonder & sickness

foetal

    read how they turn summer
    inside out turn sommer
    saults do hand springs
    looket me looket me

there in the warm salt water
so warm it is hot, almost

they could be tropical fish in a tank
a capsule before history

        outside is cold outside is weight
        outside there is air on your skin
          outside it is fatal too it is
        where they know the voices
    their mothers voices talking to them

        they are tired of waiting
    when they push off they can't
    wait the way they tumble out
      fall onto shores turn
     into birds time burns air
     we curve & bank where
    there is no warmth yet birds
  would freeze for want of weight

      or air   you wish
   you could hear your mother

lagoon

                that bay
      in Brazil
the blue shouldered
into the shoals
smoulders in opal

          & the red
running into the bay
until it looks like a heart
it should be beautiful &
from this distance is

it could be a womb, that too

    only something's wrong
      something's died
it turns & shudders beneath us
river so red it could have been
    ripped open by sharks

blood so loose the whole planet
    could be haemorrhaging

walking at night the gravel beach

Lake Winnipeg our summers sit beside
night air carries us again to things large in us
the way people since there have been people
must have brought the water in them
back to the water they came from
hung there membranous as seals for air

i guess so, that and the way we look
back through hydrogen & carbon past oxygen
and how the calcium & phosphorous
have fallen from stars
the stairs it provides through flesh for flesh
to climb pulling a bag of water behind
lug our oceans with us

the oceans churn when we hold them
to our ear
look till our necks
hurt the suns
scattered thick as sand

what do we make of this
when it spills up on the shores of night
over our heads in them our hands
wide open to find the way

home in the dark the soft
light running out onto the ground
our feet wet when we walk through

turn on two, three, four small suns
small breaths inside the room
we revolve
take the chill off the space
between stars the space left
shadows on our hands
between our fingers
where time runs through
where there is no water
we find no suns

they're gonna make a big star outta me

        vast eternity Donne wrote
          deserts of vast eternity

fast as otters & as sleek
we seek speed motion fish water

    our own bodies, bring them back
    into consonance with themselves
        wait for the lost parts
          to catch up: children
         on elevators waiting

posses waiting at the pass
stars ajinglin their faces
shiny like butter waiting
to arrest some vast eternity
pin it to their vests & wear it there
                proudly
   : badges
  they got their silver star
fish netted they have aided & abetted

who-*OA* **WH**^o**O**_A there some zealous
moustache pulling eternity over
snorting & slobbering at the bit
gods badgers gods deputies in charge
they look after arrivals & departures
they feel like something big
putting the finger on meteors
wearing stars on their chests

what he sees

it should be may the trees filling
as if there were no tomorrow instead
it is the new year it is cold and well
I do it anyway, swing the wooden cylinder
sawing the air with it there
                can be no saving now
swivel the matched eye glasses, my neck

I spy out the secrets of God's Heaven
I spy with my little eye and
my god my god what I see
what is there how can this be
         can this be

the most beautiful and delightful sight I
     rub my eyes no
              I cannot
  believe my eyes
                  have stars
        in my eyes there are spots
in my eyes and I nearly fall

                stars—thousands of them, billions
              billions and billions of tiny lights
                    no one could have seen
                        ever before
              who could have seen
              who now can believe

       stagger from the eye-piece
          head full of it look
all you have to do is look for yourselves
          look why don't you

and the moon its face lumpy as an old cow
        something sudden
  something so electric I can hardly stand
so unfixed I see a stake I try to steady
         myself at it and Bruno at it
a stinking candle howling for what he saw
                      and said

polar light

        it is something like re-entry
        something like birth if we knew
        a shudder when it hits only
        it does not hurt this time I look out
        the silence spreads forever across
                our necks & shoulders

    & in it
          such starriness
only lovers could imagine or children
darkness so deep no voice can be
    heard & then   there

tracers of bright mosquitoes
    and here and
            there
   lightning
so strong you do not think you remember
it is June and you a small child
and it is all over you and in
            that feeling
    and then

            a brilliant red
  swish of red across the sky
it could be a gash or wound
    only it is not it
       throws you inside yourself
so piercing the stars evaporate
   or you no longer see

      enormous buildings of light
      there are green ones and there is red
      and on the ends other colours

            waver so I think
      the fingers we are trying to touch
      earth is trying to brush us
      where we float in the coldest cold

          : northern lights

they could be writing something on space
something tender as breath
    & as huge

boxing day

      Dec 26/89
      flying to Chicago
  Wpg
    falls away
     a blue film

read Valentin Lebedev
Valentin Shatalov say
  how things feel
 hear them say:

   talk with
      your wife
  hear in the
      silences

   more
than she says
      more than she
   can ever
say

     . says
seeds says cold cold stars
somewhere beneath a thin film
  earth swims & breathes in

                speaks
        of love
what can we expect
                specks of life

                        how fragile
        breath is

how utterly alone how
            unutterably beautiful

viscosity

space :
       so thick
       it can
            melt you
       so thin
       you can
            smell it

                        : absorb you

my eye

that's you out there (all eyes)
fly on the sky we can see you
you little grunt there
where you sigh and bleep
you babble your bibless sleep
burp your way across the roof
through night air we long to have
you back & to let you go forever
bleating heart beating beating
at the door lemme in lemme in

what do you see child
you and your wide eyes
will you turn on your parents
turn your parents in
to charcoal in black and white
we should put you up
for adoption you

small gust in the night
chill in our dreams
lethal bubble in the blood

space walk

    door opens
          ever so
slowly

              this is it
    you are star struck
you are at your lover's door
        if you are lucky
  enemy's if not

         you are opening
             your eyes
     in the dark
      you know
something is there

               — sunlight
     slams into you

it is not slim   or tender
      but you must be
  careful
     this is your first time
ever

        do not move
        a muscle
          be still
         be very still

```
you are very small
         do not move
   at all
         or too quickly
            if you do not
   watch your step
            you will lose
everything

                  you will be dazed
                  one of these days
                         you &
                  your dazzled face
                         will turn
            in to a moon
```

visitations

all night the storm
something frightening in the trees
heavy darkness & lights
wobble off & on
past sleep & thunder
runs through easy as a horse farting
artillery all night near Amiens

in the morning the yard
a hard emerald & robins
littered with leaves & twigs

bones my daughter who slept through says
fingers the spacemen left behind

strolling in the garden

    the first ones shoot up
    the garden we planted
             beets radishes and cucumbers
        the peas come fast
  out of the soil with a fat stem
          and leaves wrapped
      tight as my daughters fist
don't go daddy please don't
after we left the wheat and oats
flares of palegreen light

whenever there was a shock they would shake
and I would remember wind on the fields at home
and in some of the fields stooks where the wind blew
and it's your face and hair and you smell wheat

    every morning first thing I would be off
    into the Oasis, Anatoli still asleep
    says for gods sake Lebedev what's the rush
    you never grew a weed back home

    fair enough but there I would be deltas below
    hands broken open rivers where they suck
    from the sea leaves Kuril saw shine
    when parts are gone as some would say deleted

and I am strolling into the garden
happy as a mutt light and chlorophyll
puffing into my face I soak in it
                    shake it all over
Aleksei come on in Aleksei
                    the air is fine

we even had fish they would swish past plants
planets whole galaxies washing over us
and we are sorry when they begin
to die we lie feeding feeling better
somehow beside the thin stems
        we walk in our grove
            like the first people
                        alone   & not caring
    except for home

preface

the clamour of those who put them there

Russell L. Schweickart claims it was not
glamour or not just that it was
numbing exhausting a lot of it
"simulations, training sessions,
mission rules meetings [they
flew missions glued nouns
together], and so forth" Russell
L. Schweickart says they would
climb into small gleams
darkness contains and they would

               blast "your soft pink
body off the planet atop a towering
pillar of flame" they flew missions
on pillars of flames, a glimpse
of poetry "How ordinary
it seemed" a soft pink body
propped, popped into space more & more

pink bodies why pink? burst into space
sweet as candied popcorn
Russell is candid about this

all those all Americans bending
blinded by the screens panels
thank the lord for American know how
in fervency promote Russian repression
space is not cold enough nor
empty enough anywhere they cannot hear
Valentin Lebedev Aleksandr Aleksandrov
Aleksei Leonov the simple elegance
what they say their homely talk
how the blue world goes
        round
                      & round
  & round

winter to winter night to night
children   gardens   sun   wind
    rain   snow   home
a tenderness when you read moves you
     into the stars people
hold and burn within themselves
               & around you

imagine something so slack
so lacking they speak blast-off
gauges instrument packages trans
lunar insertion the imperatives
of exploration a syntax stiff
from catechism a chasm of words
imagine what foul dust floats
in the wake of their dreams

how they wish they could spring
from the laboured and arthritic prose
spare some spiral of breath
they wait for & because they do not
marvel do not let themselves know
what would touch us do not reach
tenderly to feel the face
on the stars & the waters

what failure of heart the stars
do not fill or fire their heads
do not heat up seem almost to burn out
something the imagination strains
after to find light so new
it is budded light so pure
they can drink it down in wonder

how to find something very old
some thing so fresh they would laugh to hear
they have never found and need now
more than ever in an awkward
stumble toward grace

bonnie

    no it's not an orange
     it's many colours
    & we are peeling it
   wearing away the coat
   the abrasions we take to it
     as if we were
    making marmalade

    till she's a whole new
      ball game
    this belle of the ball
      blue lady
     till she's lepral
   spectral as moon & as bony

two skulls grinning at each other
their lonely dance in a darkened ballroom
there on the dark end &

 what will you think
what about your bonnie lass then
when she's not up to scratch

will you sing still to her
will you stand under a saxophone moon
      o come back blue
     lady come back don't
       be blue anymore

home game

when one falls silent out we go
earth dropping behind we sail
into darkness fall silent a moment
when day foams in our wake
one false move & we're goners

        for two days we look   —nothing
        can't spot it she's dug a hole
        in space the bitch
                        -nothing doing
    and then
           ,there

    Chuck shouts there she is
sure enough right at the horizon
flashes in the sun and we're on

        out the door and   ,that's her
hurtling away from the high cold night
                blank as a rock
    the vast melancholy of that

        she'll help us make it
    through the night so far
and close we catch our breath
as if suddenly a shirt were too tight

she's in bad shape all right this momma
taken a terrible beating
skin peeling away in scabs she's quite a sight
and not a peep out of her not a fart
even her eyes are closed her face shut inside

on the small table we know
there is bread & salt inside
    & there is no one there
the emptiness of an empty cabin
warmth once bounced in   & voices

little pig little pig let us in you old tart
show a little heart hey lady

all jowls and belly and we pat her
on the bum listen old lady
you sick or just goofing off or what
we been too long in the pub she
gives us the cold shoulder a deadly cold

    look for days at her
    stomach and cabling peer
    flash lights in her face
    wake up momma wake up
    c'mon old lady

    reattach her to the sun
    snap on the lights in the kitchen
    she thinks in & we think
    it's about time so
    we make ourselves at home
    settle in for the night

    warmed by the hair on her
chinny chin chin we worm our way
    into her heart take her by storm
    by morning she'll be howling
    with delight, momma will

little momma little pig

rock pickers

till others reach out burglars of space
snap the locks off
stars pin & number

they are bagmen in a big world
click them off with tinsnips

they could be picking
the gates of heaven

carry stars away in burlap
light hurting their hands
hot gasses in their eyes
feel it all the way
into their feet burning

it dawns on us

1,   2,   4 ,   8,   16,
                              sun

                    sets
16 suns   rise

            every day

                        plip
                                    -it's up

                plip
                    -down

sun an echo in our eyes

                & when it is
            down
                    we are
    past the lights Japan gives us
                                & then

    the Pacific
            swallows us whole
                rum on its breath

                                I wait
                        man clinging
                to a runaway milk truck
                it is out of control
                and the lights are out

          wait for dawn
                blip in a film
           when it's over
          or runs too fast

     your stomach floats
   all the cells
in your body
  racing acing acing acing
        much too
  fast ast ast ast

our old man's a dustman

their ponderous revolving
doors at Eaton's in deepest winter
galaxies some times stumble into one another

something clumsy something touching
      those heavy wheelings
round one another tidal forces

pull out scarves of gas dust stars
you in your red scarf the cold wind
your breath on the air flares
wild arcs far into the system
far as the eye can see & further

        at the centre
        pots of hydrogen
        silently boiling

      air so terrifyingly thin
it could be a nylon pulled over our head
& there is the cold & darkness of forever

Magellan, all the stars
when he slid south

      all the stars in his head
      "he understood dead reckoning
      and celestial navigation
      better than anyone in the world"

      Pigafetta said, and told
      how the men turned on Magellan
      mutinied under the stars
      when they were on their way

around the globe 5 small ships
their provisions cut by 2/3
crooked suppliers? saboteurs?
they scraped the bottom of heaven
scoured it on their way to somewhere
they all wanted to see the stars
had they all gone to see the stars then

Magellan on his way the torturous straits
before him Magellan heading south
watches the sky where it eats
stars out of his hands & eyes
the very heaven where it configured
his mind since a boy is sliding
out of position the sky a series
giant wheels there in the Milky
Way toppling over into new shapes
his ships reel under

        all the stars in his head
        when he would stare
        the immense darkness
        would slowly shift & fold
the old patterns falling out near
patterns climbing into his brain
the strange southern sky

       and then, gradually, two
hazy patches scratch onto his retina
though he blinks they are still there
one smaller than the other
radiant lint on the heavens
his sight clouds with them, blurs over
he could be waking, sleep in his eyes
        the enormous bright dust
            catches his brain
beyond all his ship's reckoning

  something in him is forever
  something occluded something beautiful
                    frighteningly clear

such a stream of stars could be sailors' hair
streaming in wind their faces where they look up
          white as moons, as mutinous

  the sudden stroke he must have felt
        when it hit

                did he too dream of home
a warm bed
            a woman's touch,   in morning
                did he wonder
         would he ever   touch earth

                        & later when they found
                        the dazzling birds of paradise
                                    that flew forever
                        over the earth inside green
                            inside whistles of air
                        did he dream
                                of home
                        small light on a table
                          a homely touch

held

    bounced off the membrane
             that held us in
    skin that keeps us
    from blackness & death

    winds scatter across the stars
    steer us into enormous chasms
    we slide our dreams into
    grass and woods and

        the canary islands
        silver so luminous
    you think of wiping it off
              its wetness

navigation

    learned to be at home
           in the stars
  the lines we would
      take from them

          pouring through
  the dark cold waters
      we flew by
  the stars in our heads

the squeeze earth puts you in

        when you land
the body relaxing on itself
the ease that falls upon you

at first there is a
  dub a-**DUB DUB**adub **DUBDUB**
                /like that
   planes when they hit
            too hard
     only fast   , much faster
tremors run over you
       shaky as heart beat
             & then

  when you land
          ,softly
   & rock
you are on the other end

     then still
      & then
                  - faces
   sweet smell of rain
   on you   & wind
           so moved
     you cannot
   move
         you can actually smell
           the wind

                    your whole body
            feels swollen,   wobbly
    as a new baby
                you cannot
        move
                    your arms & legs
                        & the earth
        when you land
        where you step
                    trembly

                under your first
    steps

impaled on a trajectory

yes we know earth
is imperilled impelled on
mad dreams we ourselves fuel
that it is not well
there is a terrible sickness
that will lead to death
the earth is about to fall
where it sits &
splatter on space below

& yet we feel a home
sickness a longing
none of us has ever felt

want to fall back
along the cracks rains make
millennia more let the rains
wash our bones let birds
fall into our throats & out
let us let this happen

we want to dance
the days we have left
what we have we must hold
careful as breath itself
though it all will perish
let us perch a little while
we are tired of flying

              we will return
       sick of heart sick for home
       our hearts full of it
       we would touch earth
       before, until, our dust like Niagara
       crashes back to the end

the men in the moon

yes the dried apricots one of us
with a pocket full of little moons

my daughter Katya's teddy bear
we tether to its ear we know
it can hardly hear us the little runt
but we hang onto all the same
hands steady on her gift
we hang from an elastic band
it drops to us where we swim
among the honey stars hungry for home

       remember the story
when we were children our fathers
would scrape sound across the floor
             and tell us
the lost children the little boy
the small moons scraps of yellow
sounds he drops on the way
          and later they follow
  home cold and lonely
              in the night

the orbits of planets the sphere of the stars

there is a shaft of light straight through heaven and earth like a rainbow only brighter and clearer for this light does not shift it holds heaven and from its ends hangs a spindle which causes all the orbits to revolve in a huge whorl hollowed out with a second smaller one fitting exactly into it and this one is hollowed out to hold a third and the third to hold a fourth until there are eight each with another inside like a set of mixing bowls. their rims show in perfect circles around the brilliant shaft and the largest and outermost rim is filled with colours the seventh is the brightest the sixth illuminated by the seventh and the others yellow and white and red and white.

the whole spindle revolves with a single motion swings through the heavens but within it the seven inner circles roll slowly, more and more slowly as the circles become smaller and on top of each circle there is a siren carried round with it Circe singing one note and the eight notes together make up one scale. and sailing all around them are three others on thrones or golden branches, these three in white dresses and voices. one sings of things past, another of things present, the third of things to come, and from time to time spin in perfect rhyme the outer rim and inner rims like potters throwing pots, or human hearts.

—adapted from Desmond Lee's translation of *The Republic*

alluvial

we have seen
islands that draw water to them
lakes that lock silver look red
clay deserts crevices with long purple
combed into them or the air
ancient craters blue from snow

we have seen the Amazon
pulped fibre and clouds someone's shaken
out a pillow and paired lakes
they could be ovaries they flow
into Lake Winnipeg receives them
fish through fallopian tubes

rivers through plains red as the insides
animals have coastal tides
could have fallen off vases
crusted with day the long Nile
snakes swim mountains in Iran
bony as trilobites old
as the earth and the hot indigestion

the Sahara curdles the Gambia
an aorta of hot gold

Kepler

I am Johannes Kepler keeper of the numbers and the stars
born inside religious war and broken joints
and I have seen bodies cracked open on hate and hunger
my own aunt roasted alive at the stake and my mother
almost my wife burnt away on a fever in war
men in my times torn apart by mares eyes singed out
mercury in the wrong conjunction the moon a splot of blood
my father Lutheran himself go as mercenary in mud and snow
he killed Protestants in the Netherlands beat my mother
the sky crowded it seemed with comets or deserted
a thousand disasters "against the stars"
ships at sea the wreckage in their wake
the whole world it seemed without mercy and burning

    and now I turn my eye to other lands the seas
    swarming over us swimming with bright fish
    kippers I could say but do not
    I am Kepler sick man I do not
    make jokes they think except they are
    the stars and I a skipper sailing through
    spirits direct and turn in the wake singing to us
    we are skippers in a bright bright sea
    though Tycho whirrs me round him like a slingshot

I have seen the turnings of stars
the perfect tunings God has inscribed there
the heavens humming with tops and I have seen
storms wash over coasts and whole cities
storms that swoop peasants into revolutions
the planets wide murmurings have marked
how the Turks glimmer in blood at the horizon
murmurs in our hearts and I have studied the red planet
steadied it in its bloody socket
  one day, before, with my students
   it is July 19, 1595,
     and I am speaking
       it is all I can do
    not to say finders keepers
      but that would be silly
   my fingers where they point   & pick

      nets I say   nests
    conjunctions   Saturn and Jupiter
  pass through eight zodiacs from one
  trine to another trine and it is thus I
  inscribe circle within circle
  triangle with triangle look I say
  how it all falls into place
    it is all there everything
      so elegantly   untangles
  and there is something like a tingle
  only giant and slow in enormity such elegance
  such beauty my children don't you see
  the birds the swift bright birds how they
       wheel & cry

how the earth in its orbit measures all things
how within its dodecahedron Mars circles
and in Mars' tetrahedron a circle holds Jupiter
and Jupiter cubed contains a circle Saturn is

the sweep the beauty of it I had hoped to find
and I write Galileo to tell him so, later
all the long slow couplings and uncouplings

look now how it all fits together look I say
                        it locks
                                      & unlocks

       here

                          & here

& here

                                 & here

listen you can hear murmurs of the cosmos
murmurings in our hearts children
an icosahedron from earth puts Venus in a circle
Venus within an octahedron puts Mercury into another circle
that is the beauty of it do you not see my children
souls that steer the seven stars perfect as birds or fish
only the circles bulge to ellipses and there are rumours
there are wars and tumours loom into sight in the sky
                                  what is this

                    I, Kepler, feel so
         helpless
                and so stricken

you have the reasons for the seven planets
         how one body fits so
exactly into place among the others how god moves
in perfect harmonics don't you see the morning
stars singing together the luminous signs

over the broken and bloodied body
singed wings the winds with cinders soldiers stir
        how Europe is   a little girl
      bends   to kiss Africa
       its severed head
the weeping house earth has become
                  the shingles we crouch under loud with blood

they wow the earth

       stars a scatter of dandruff
       : : rocks in the interlake
whole fields strewn with rocks

    stars squirm   : :
the wet hair of night
matted & tangled there
   stars seek the way

      home earth serene as an Easter egg
        clear with eternity
                  stars
     fragrant after
   shave
       splashed all over the place
all over their face

  :

    ;

•

          ,

   stars frequent the place
   every night come out
    hang around
  & show their stuff

vacuum

never believed
what they said
when they said
it was magic &
we must do it

all these numb
ers & instrume
nts this talkg
ravity & caps
ules & suspic
ions i never
liked the ta
lk of metals
& me cha nic
sta king & b
eat ingo nly
wok eon eda y
fo un d Yuri
bi gsm ile
plas te red
allov erhis
fac eth is
bi gloo nie
g rint oo thy
a sac owir
ubm ye yes

ha-ay Valentin
riding around
this big crow
ha-ay wake up
ya big goon

        crazy Valentin flying
        past the moon
        crazy as a kid
        on an electric broom

leaving

*

      three of them
    & they are walking
        there is a red horizon & a sun
squashed in it a mandarin orange &
    it is bleeding and above it
        purple it looks like stratified rock
they walk into & there are three towers
          & a little one

    there are three
their backs to us & in their hands
    left hands something that
      could be lunch baskets
        they could be kids
their mothers stuffed in snowsuits

      the camera is low & there is light
behind & so they look
    powerful in their shadows   & strange
        they could be gods

**

    except Aleksandr says it is breathing
you can see her breath where it comes down
her body is slim & elegant her skin you touch
there she is in the red wind she waits

she is dressed in a gown
white as frost we are the first
she is waiting & we are walking
toward her three of us three towers
a sky that is red & purple

nemesis

"Life stays pretty much as is until something disastrous happens, and then life changes fast." —Jonathan Weiner, *Planet Earth*

some say there is a death star
that every 26 million years or so
it lunges back to the sun
a twin returning home
perfect orphan the very sort
lost soul you would expect
it is small dark far off a dwarf
but it is big enuff it will do
& it may fall back before we do
                     , to the sun

   on its way back maybe it
     loses its way & stumbles on the dark
crashes into the Oort cloud
comets where they snuggle
interstellar night

         twist an ancient myth &
                  /out of nowhere
                      something
       crashes
    right out of the blue
                : a big rock
   falls from the sky
wham into the earth unfurls
dust and cold around the earth
easy as a slip slides your body

the dinosaurs topple over from darkness
darkness rubs their eyes out
they are wrecked hangars birds fly from
a hunger snaps from their spines
clothes lines in winter & wind
a counter song opposing dance

      there is quartz shocked
      as if it were a nuclear blast

      a catastrophe yes a cata-
      strophe a down turn over turn a twist

only from the giant shadows
their bodies cast or once cast
& numb as rocks they now fall into
small squints of fur run
out into our cerebra & thumbs
         stretch out
into the hands we
               all winter
          stretch out each day
        to each other whatever
            fires we can find

      our lives on this planet
        Derek Ager says
      are the lives of soldiers
        long stretches of boredom
    & then short periods of terror

this only world

  what I remember most   -the silence
  most of all an enormous silence
    unlike any I have ever known
  and we would listen the way you listen
   to a baby in its crib and you fear
    it is not alive or breathing
 and you cannot hear for the longest time

 silence so vast and deep I begin to hear
 my own body the swish in the vessels
   my heart I can hardly believe
  the muscles move and there is
   the rustle shirts and vests
   make when you are dressing
  in morning I hear them rubbing
  when they move over each other
   the way we move our silence

settlers I have heard on the Canadian prairie
moved into a huge silence wavered
on air there like birds in a desert
& emptiness not to be believed
       tumbled past

and the stars my god the stars far more
than ever I would have thought
I do not know what but this sky
is so black a deep black but it is
bright with sun the earth is

a small bright light so breath
-takingly blue & white its
gentle cloud of breath
dear earth dear child
        so all alone the home we left
          the earth so round I never knew
                how round how small
              until I saw the earth

        passing
time

in the end we listened
    to:

        folk songs
          sounds of
         rain
          thunder
         birds
              mainly robins
             many robins
     singing

        homely
        sounds
   sounds of home

Apollo II What They Will Leave Behind

It is Saturday, July 19, 1969. The papers say three Americans (Neil A. Armstrong, Col. Edwin E. Aldrin Jr., and Lt.-Col. Michael Collins) will leave the command ship, Columbia, drop inside a small craft, the Eagle, onto a part of the moon called the Sea of Tranquility.

No one will see the separation because a commercial communications satellite has failed. No one will know quite what will happen when the craft, which they also call a LEM, gets to the moon. Thomas O'Toole says it looks more like a giant insect than a bird, says its face is pulled open by surprise or alarm. Says it might settle so gently on the moon's face it could be a bird touching down. This will happen on Saturday afternoon (3:19 p.m. CDT).

The papers say that much of the payload will be abandoned. They will leave a variety of equipment and litter. Among the items are the following:

1. Rod support for Solar Wind Composition Experiment.
2. American Flag.
3. Two pairs of lunar boots.
4. A Laser Ranging Retro-Reflector.
5. One very expensive LM descent stage, 31 feet in diameter and approximately 10 feet high.
6. Westinghouse black and white lunar camera.
7. A gnomon.
8. One of two Portable Life Support System (PLSS) units.
9. Also discarded will be one PLSS feedwater collection bag for measurement of coolant water not used.

10. One extension handle for use with various tools, a scoop and one pair of tongs.
11. A Passive Seismology Experiment (PSE) to measure lunar quakes.

Other items left behind and not shown include armrests from the LM cabin, two still cameras and a motion picture camera, used food bags and used fecal containers and urine bags.

Meantime Thor Heyerdahl and his crew of six leave a battered reed boat they named Ra. They are on their way across the Atlantic, trying to prove the Egyptians could have sailed to America over 4,000 years ago. Sharks prevent the crew from completing the voyage.

When he gets there Neil Armstrong will say early Monday morning (1:21 a.m. CDT) when he steps on the moon's face to get his bucket of rocks he's taken a step.

He will also leave a few stamps on which the United Nations is depicted, except they will never get on the spacecraft because US Mission Control will say they cannot find time to decontaminate the card sent by Thant on July 11. Armstrong will do this though some members of Congress do not approve of including the UN material. He will not leave a copy of the preamble to the UN charter. The stamps total 93 cents in value. They depict the UN flag, the UN seal, the preamble to the charter, the international year for human rights, peaceful uses of outer space and peace through international law.

Armstrong and Edwin (Buzz) Aldrin will walk easily, even run and jump. When they plant the American flag they will salute it. They will talk with President Nixon in the White House, then face the camera and salute him. Pope Paul will hail them as "conquerors of the moon." Headlines will say they struck paydirt.

The footprints will remain on the moon for half a million years.

Outside the Manned Space Center auditorium in Houston, as the Eagle lands, black demonstrators carry signs saying "41 cents a day is not enough."

Deuteronomy prescribes God's wrath for anyone who worships the moon.

A Babylonian legend tells how a god rapes the moon, then replaces her with his son Sin.

Michael Collins says, though the papers do not report it, the moon does not look very friendly or inviting, wonders what they are doing there.

Later, when Alan Bean arrives, he will look at earth and think how far, far away it is. James Irwin will stand among mountains and canyons, wonder how all alone Adam and Eve must have felt.

dried apricots

dried apricots we found dried apricots today
and I thought when I was young
I would watch the moon and that's what
I thought the moon is a dried apricot

my mother would say that's nice Aleksandrov
and she would tell me stories there would be
snow and cold at the door
you would drink or smells of gardens
in spring when everything's wet from rain
and you get stuck once in your rubber boots
and she pulls you out, scolding

once she said Aleksandr look and there was
a small bird in her hand a robin I think
or a yellow bird so bright I thought
it was the sun there my mother held in her hand

    and now this bag of little moons
    some friend has smuggled onto the ship
    it's as if we are closer to home
    earth whirls in fluff and deserts red as icing
    giant eye balls swirl to tropical storms
    I have never been to but something happens
    when there is ice laid on a teal
    table clean as mother's linen in Hudson Bay
    and Moscow and it is winter

        thunder rain the singing of birds the earth turning
          green under us and blue blue as Anishka's eyes

all this seems now so very far away
as if it happened a long time ago
    "and we no longer there
      and it is not known
       when we will be again"

theres Gary

           - white moth
so bright in the sun
                   he flutters
    slowly

        held there in math
the same math that put us here
                 /same myth
    he is drawn there
 we were drawn
some sweet compulsion

      parabolas the neurons
  send him on
         he thuds & bounces
  off almost
     loses
his balance or balances
   there where the light
         sends him
suspends him in its veins
light varnishes his face & we vanish
do not know when we will come back
        or if ever

letters

        in all that
    you had time to listen
    sounds of your thoughts going away

sometimes loose newspapers in winter
sometimes your hand over paper
your hair at night collar undone
night and day thoughts crawling to you

sometimes the way your body would
kick in you think by god it's a furnace
lungs rumbling away with air & it's good
the blood chugging the system
it all gets blurred   & rubbed

        & i write
                letters
     dear father
       dear linda
  one letter after the other
    what are you   doing
     dangling away   on the afternoon
   listen   dear daughter   gangly as april
when will you   wake   how is the baby i will
see you soon dear people where are you phil
what do you look like elaine son uncle allen cousin
how are you aunt dear meggie my love my mother

       they never reach you
       they never do

             dear god   where are you
              you wish you could   now
    it is   far off write listen listen where
                     & they could
                 see you
     there at the far borders parks are in
                      wave
                   ,palely
         take care you write take care

                       write them
          where are you are you   how if only
                 i know   yes   letters
                    what are you saying
       your faces going
                  i will see you soon
            & please write thinking of you
                               dear god
                   how are you

foundry

earth sweaty from day one
squints all day squats all night
in its swarthiness it is
a foundling swaddled in darkness

        earth wheezes darkness
        grazes its shoulder

        stars where speed rubs
        spray off into night

earth that blue-eyed bitch
spinny with its own strength
all its days wobble on its spindly axis
swats all night long at the stars

scanning the heavens

      moon   is a stone
          set in a
sling shot

         earth swings
               round
           & round
   its head

             the whistles & roars
     oceans of hormones
                 pound our ears
          wash up
              the estuaries
                 we are lost
    continents in flood

          moon is an ovary
          moon is a stone
              hurtling
     in space
we are lost   continents in flood

   moon is a stone

hatched

we would joke when the door would jerk
open and pop out we would go just like that
without a hitch, got rather good at it
lighter than hats we would dangle
spiders in night someone unlocked
laughter and someone would say

    hey Georgi or look Vladimir
    we laid an egg this is the goose
    that laid the golden egg
            just our luck

and you would feel like a child
chilled all of a sudden when you looked
    the line slack and wriggling

a snake so slick there it would be
the door to the hatch in a night
so deep you could find your dreams
    switched on   & glowing
the lamp hitched to your back yard
        & you
    your friends over beer
lumps that fill the dark,
    the chocolate pudding

    the door to the hatch shining
like my gramma's door in the country

        your children's doors
        plump with it
        flowing with light

& you have been drunk

       the weight drained from you & light
          headed slept on the top
        & had every thought
of returning & been stricken
  to silence   on the shores
as if you had a stroke or fallen
  in love   is this what it is

              you have drunk lights
                  spilled at the window
            earth   swimming within
                 its black   night

    bright globe
bounced   out of the classroom
                    every morning
  our teacher spun   & stopped
    & what is   this country
where is this
      what   is this
          creak of chalk
wood   your head turning
all the shapes   the beautiful shapes

      this is what
       i have   wanted
                          :

sailing   ships

                                   +

))

;

( )

!

! ∫

"

-

! !

. ,+

    red ,sails,
        & yellows
              /like that
& peacock blue

             all i could ever
        see   or feel
         all i could   keep
with me

                        all this   i may lose
                  i may remember

space colony

    how dreadful to hurtle for years
    & years to hurdle years inside
    some tube some shell a skull
    they call a ship a loneliness
    they call adventure

        where could you go
        what could you see

never to visit green never to walk rivers home
never to take smells on your hands off tomatoes
stronger than sex feel the sun on your back
never to call on the stories your grandmother tells
never to feel snow on your face never
smell burning grass saskatoons when you eat
never to walk over rocks into water
none of these things not even to watch baby orioles
at the sprinkler dance round their bones and drink

        as if you could catapult
        your heart into eternity
        your body into nowhere
        who ever could want this
        leaving yourself behind
    the weather below you, happening

Eugene Cernan

what ever soundings you take
        from pole to pole
    the earth is
            surrounded
rounded by blackness though
          you are looking through
              sun-
    light there is only light

if the sunlight
      has some thing some flake
                to stick on
      or flick to
shine when the sun shines through

      space is black as oil all
            because the light doesn't
strike anything the light doesn't

           strike
  anything
      so
             all you
see is
      a black sea of light
  leak past   lakes and lakes of it

      a lack of light
             unless
      you get
  in the way

```
we do not see
                one another
           unless we stand
    in the way and the light
         gets stopped

           when the stars stop
    i think
                our breath does too
```

home again

to come back to
        dogs barking
  sharp in morning
    coffee &
        someone
calling for you
brick warm in the sun
    & bread

      your son's sweatshirt
      after hockey

    the sound of you
moving sweetly to day   or to love
    your body on mine

      how when we were away
  the pull we fight we cling to
   grand mother lover we love
& though it appears never leave her
   think we will wave to her
  circle in delight & adoration
    but how will she know
      we are waving
  where death in our hearts
      waits for us

earth when it gives
          mushy in march as oatmeal
        scrape of wind
  & the phone
rings you to come back
        to your senses
           come back
  to earth

how good to be
          returned to ourselves

    this our ever flowing
    ever flowering earth

    how fine how new
    the only home we have
    or will have ever